AVOIDING MILLION DOLLAR MISTAKES

The 3 Things You MUST Do To Sell Your Business For Big Money

ANDREW LONGCORE

www.SellSmallBiz.com

AVOIDING MILLION DOLLAR MISTAKES

Copyright © 2016 by Andrew S. Longcore

This is a work of nonfiction. Any resemblance to actual persons, organizations or events are purely coincidence and unintentional.

This publication is not intended for use as a source of legal or accounting advice. The author and publisher want to stress that the information contained herein may be subject to varying federal, state and local laws and regulations. All users are advised to retain their own competent counsel to determine what federal, state or local laws or regulations may apply to the user's particular business.

All rights are reserved with the author, including the right of reproduction in whole or in part in any form.

ISBN: 1-5354-4312-X
ISBN-13: 978-1535443128

DEDICATION

" *Kristy Lynn, no one has ever directly or indirectly pressed me into action as you do every day. I am who I am and I will be a better version of myself tomorrow because of you. I could not imagine arriving at any destination without you by my side. I will love you 'til the end.* "

Contents

PART I: THE BIG IDEA 1

   CHAPTER 1: LET'S GET GOING 2

   CHAPTER 2: THE WRONG END OF BIG PROBLEMS 5

   CHAPTER 3: MY SOLUTION 7

   CHAPTER 4: ORGANIZATION 10

PART II: MISTAKE #1:
YOU HAVE ALL THE TIME IN THE WORLD 13

   CHAPTER 5: YOU DON'T HAVE TO GO HOME, BUT YOU CAN'T STAY HERE 14

PART III: MISTAKE #2:
EVERY BUSINESS CAN BE SOLD FOR SOMETHING 17

   CHAPTER 6: DRIVING THE VALUE BUS 18

   CHAPTER 7: OPTIMIZATION 20

   CHAPTER 8: MANAGEMENT TEAM 22

   CHAPTER 9: CUSTOMER/VENDOR AGREEMENTS 25

   CHAPTER 10: EMPLOYEES 32

   CHAPTER 11: LITIGATION/POTENTIAL LITIGATION 45

   CHAPTER 12: STRATEGIC ACQUISITION 48

   CHAPTER 13: LAST BUT NOT LEAST 56

   CHAPTER 14: VALUE CONCLUSION 60

PART IV: MISTAKE #3:
YOU DON'T HAVE TO KNOW ABOUT THE STRUCTURE OF A DEAL UNTIL IT'S TIME TO SELL 63

CHAPTER 15: EXPRESSION OF INTEREST 65

CHAPTER 16: LETTER OF INTENT 67

CHAPTER 17: DON'T GET MARRIED TO THE WRONG BUYER 70

CHAPTER 18: DUE DILIGENCE 72

CHAPTER 19: PURCHASE AGREEMENT 74

CHAPTER 20: POST CLOSING 79

PART V: MISTAKE #4:
YOU HAVE IT MADE IN THE SHADE AFTER YOU SELL YOUR BUSINESS 81

CHAPTER 21: THE NEED TO BE NEEDED 83

CHAPTER 22: PERSONAL FISCAL RESPONSIBILITY 85

PART VI: NOW WHAT 87

ABOUT THE AUTHOR 90

PART I

THE BIG IDEA

1 Let's Get Going

Here is the big idea in less than 100 words:

> You are a business owner who has done little to no planning for leaving your business. You have no idea where to start or how to increase the value of your business. The process seems foreign and overwhelming to you. I am here to tell you the formula for a successful exit from your company is not complex:
>
> *Time + Strategic Improvements + Knowledge = Success.*

I was not meant to write this book. I was not supposed to be sitting in this chair. The degrees on my wall were meant for someone else. In fact, you shouldn't be having this conversation with me right now. But some higher power in the universe flipped a number of switches and bounced me around like a pinball to land me here to help you.

One of my earliest memories comes from when I was in elementary school. Someone had the perverse idea to put 8-year-old kids in front of the entire school to give a short speech on what they were going to be when they grew up. I could have told you at that point in time, motivational speaker was not an option, because my knees were shaking with fear behind that microphone.

I remember feeling like I was outside my body as the words creeped past my lips. It was like I going through the motions, but I was not actively participating because the fear of public speaking was so powerful. I somehow got through my entire speech on how I was going to be an orthopedic surgeon (Yes, I was that specific with my intentions even back then) and didn't do so bad. At least none of my classmates ridiculed me for making an ass of myself, but that could have been because they were all filled with the same fear and they did not know if they performed well either.

There it was for the world to hear. My goal of becoming an orthopedic surgeon. And that's how it was through high school. I even volunteered on the weekends at the local hospital restocking linens, wheel-chairing people around and filing papers because I thought it would get me exposure to the culture and it would look pretty good on my resume.

Even going to college, I lined up all of my classes to be on the pre-med track. Then the day came where I was told I needed to pick a specific discipline to major in. For the life of me I could not narrow it down. They all seemed so boring. Biology. Chemistry. Physiology. It did not matter to me because the thought of years of having to sit through any more of those boring classes made each one blur into "Want to Gouge My Eyes Out-ology" to me.

There was a solution to my dilemma. My college offered a seminar course with the dean that helped find which major best fit your aptitude. Despite this being presented as a solution, it turned out to not be a solution at all. Or at least I didn't see it as a solution. The dean told me, after all of the aptitude and personality tests, that I was not meant to be a doctor. He told me I was a much better fit as a lawyer. What?! I wanted to be a doctor for as long as I could remember. Who wants to be an attorney? This guy was nuts.

He convinced me to take one history class and see how it fit. He also said that there were certain lawyers that work closely with the medical profession and so I could perhaps still have my toe in the medical arena. Looking back, I have to wonder if he was talking about those attorneys that get the title "ambulance chaser," because that was never an option for me.

Needless to say, I fell in love with that one history class and that led me to focus on business transactions in law school. Everything was easy street from there, right? I didn't know becoming a business attorney would create the biggest problem I had ever faced in my life.

2 The Wrong End of Big Problems

Let me be the first to break some news that many of you already know. The practice of law does not properly serve small- and medium-size businesses. Now I am sure many of you have worked with an attorney before. How many of you were really impressed and saw immense value from the services you received? How many of you called that attorney again and again to get advice and bounce ideas off of? How many of you hated the bill that followed or were floored when you heard the hourly rate?

Here is the problem: The firms that focus on a niche (or are big enough to have departments that focus on one area of the law) generally are really good at what they do and thus you have to pay top dollar for their representation. The firms that are less focused may be more affordable, but you rarely get someone with the expertise you need.

When you look at the organizational structure of any Fortune 500 Company, they always have a general counsel or a chief legal officer. Donald Trump has had Michael Ross beside him for over 20 years. Warren Buffett has had Charlie Munger for even longer. Clearly these business behemoths and titans of industry see the counsel from an attorney as invaluable in their business. How is a small business or even a middle market business supposed to get that kind of counsel when the options are eyebrow raising fees or working with someone who will be handling a DUI case for another client after you leave his office?

Finally the kicker to the problem with the practice of law is many attorneys refer to themselves as "attorney and counselor" but they forget (or they don't know) what being a *counselor* means. Many an attorney, in order to prove his value, will make unnecessary changes to documents or advise the client in a way that gets in the way more than anything.

Think of it this way: if you send a software licensing agreement to your attorney, who reviews it, tells you that it looks acceptable and sends you an invoice for a few hours of service, do you see any value in what you are paying for? Now what if that same document comes back to you with all kinds of red marks, dire warnings and proposed alternative language. Suddenly you can see that this guy is well worth paying because you almost fell into some kind of business pitfall. But are you getting any real value with the second option? I mean the deal you agreed to before your attorney got involved must have had some level of benefit to you because it made it to the contract stage. If your attorney is blowing up that deal, does it really help your business out?

If a buyer wants to buy and a seller wants to sell, why should anyone get in the way of that process? A client deserves to make an informed decision with a full understanding of the potential risks. But the ultimate decision should be up to the client and not the attorney. After all, it's the client's business and not the attorney's, right?

3 My Solution

There was only one option left: I had to build the right firm for small- and medium-size business owners. One that not only gave them the same concentrated, expertise that they need, but also a business model that fit their budget. Those business owners that see that they can build something great, that will survive them and will help their family, employees and community for years and years after they retire, love the idea of having their own general counsel for their business who is pushing their business in a direction to leave the lasting legacy they envision. And that is our number one goal: build and preserve the legacies of business owners.

We do this by setting up long-term plans for our clients. We act as their general counsel or chief legal officer. We find out where they have been, where they are at and where they want to go. After that, we put together a plan that fits within their budget to ensure they have access to us, receive the services they need and achieve their goals.

At my firm we are counselors first and foremost. We are not in the order business. I don't take orders like a waiter and I don't give orders like a dictator. This book gives you a glimpse into a few of the proven methods that we advise our clients on to help them grow the value and create demand for their business. This will allow them to successfully transition away from their business.

I will be the first to point out that my philosophy and the content in this book are not for everyone. It might not be for you. You might love being so needed by your business that you can't take a peaceful vacation. You may have no interest in pursuing other ventures or retiring. You may believe that you will never have a health issue or some other reason that forces you to leave your business. You might not care about the legacy you leave behind or what happens to your employees after you turn out the lights that one last time. You may be happy with a business that covers paying your bills for your current lifestyle and you don't want to worry about what tomorrow may bring. Heck, there are a few of you out there that think a successful exit from your business is all luck and no matter what you do it's out of your hands. If you are in any of these categories, I would implore you to read on in hopes that you change your mind. I am not delusional. Some business owners are happy with an average to below average business and have no aspirations of being great. But if you know you want to be great, this book can help you.

I was sitting in my office when I received a cold call from Bill. Bill (not his real name by the way) was a sharp business guy. He had worked in investments and transactions in New York for a number of years before returning to West Michigan to raise his family.

He had acquired the rights to be a commercial retailer for a few food products and was making a pretty good living. He actually expanded into a neighboring territory and was providing consulting services to other businesses that were selling the same products from the wholesale distributor.

Bill wanted to know if I could help him with a possible transaction. He was currently in negotiations with the wholesale distributor that supplied the products he sold. For all intents and purposes this wholesale distributor looked like a success. This was a business that was doing close to $3,000,000 in revenue and had grown 50% over the past 3 years. It had retailers across the country that exclusively purchased its products. This business was a classic case of a business that looks pretty nice from the outside, but when you dug a little below the surface you saw all kinds of issues. And Bill knew it.

Not only did Bill see this target as having huge growth potential if certain aspects were leveraged correctly, but he knew he could beat up the seller over the price during negotiations. And beat up the seller he did. By the time the dust had settled and the final check was cut, Bill had cut the original purchase price nearly in half and had cut over 40% from the professional fair market valuation of the business.

Immediately after taking possession of the business we went to work on "fixing it up" by mostly working to correct many of the holes and issues that had been leveraged in negations to lower the purchase price. Bill also went to work negotiating vendor agreements and terminating agreements with retailers that were not doing well. The result after the first year was the business had actually lost revenue but at the same time, the profits from the business had increased. In the years that followed Bill got revenue back on a growth track and profit margins are still growing.

There have been other issues in Bill's new business that were unforeseen that we have dealt with and we have more work to do on the overall plan. But less than 5 years after acquiring this business, Bill could sell it for 3 or 4 times what he purchased it for. What you need to avoid is being the guy that owned the business before Bill.

4 Organization

This book is not intended as the *end all be all* of succession planning. As pointed out above there are plenty of options to put at the end of your rainbow. Family businesses can be amazing assets that support your family for years with the right plan for transition in place. Going public has a certain celebrity and notoriety that you may desire to achieve and the profits can be huge. Your employees may be the best option for ensuring that your business will survive for years beyond your lifetime. Those are very viable exit strategies and to cover all in one book could be overwhelming (and very likely cause you to skip much of the content because of lack of relevance to your situation).

This book is intended specifically for those folks who are looking to sell their business to someone else. Many of the topics covered can have relevance to other exit strategies but it is meant to hit home with those considering this one. So everything might not be spot on for you and feel free to pick and choose what you take from the information in the following pages.

In the true spirit of this book, I would like to show you the end goal and the map we are going to follow to get there. If you are even thinking about selling your business or want to know if it might be an option, this book is meant to give you a preliminary education on the process. This is not meant to be a complete step-by-step guide. Each business is unique with its own outcome. With the knowledge you gain here you can identify where you want to go and what needs to get done.

So how are we going to get you to that point? We will go over the following:

- ☑ "Why now?" The future is far away, right? That may be true but right now is a critical time to start thinking about some very big-picture concepts or you might never get where you want to go.

- ☑ We are going to cover some points about getting your business prepared for sale. Not every business is saleable and the more value you develop in your business the more saleable it will become.

- ☑ We will look into the structure and process of a deal. You will want to know what you are getting into, right?

- ☑ We will touch on some action steps you can take right now to not only evaluate your business but also cut the learning curve of what you need to focus on right now to really drive up the value of your business.

Now that you have your map, let's roll out.

PART II

MISTAKE #1

YOU HAVE ALL THE TIME IN THE WORLD

5 You Don't Have To Go Home, But You Can't Stay Here

Can we agree on one thing right here and right now? Can we agree that every business owner leaves their business eventually? Whether you sell your business, merge your business, transfer your business, gift your business, let you employees take over or leave out the front door feet first, you are going to eventually leave your business.

With that definitive fact out in the open, the question becomes not <u>why</u> should I plan to exit my business but rather, <u>when</u> should I start planning for my exit. I am here to tell you that you can't wait for next year or next month or next week. I am not even going to tell you that you need to start planning today. I am going to tell you that you should have started when you first went into business. That's right. You are already behind.

I am not going to sugar coat the process. It does not matter if you are intending on selling your business to a third party, having your children or employees buy you out or doing an initial public offering. The process to make any of those things happen is a big, complicated mess and each has its own unique challenges. Knowing that the challenge of eating that elephant has been put in front of you, what is the best way to get that job done? You are right. One bite at a time. Making sure you have time to take all those bites is important. But is it more important than knowing which elephant you need to eat?

That is why beginning with the end in mind is so important. You give yourself as much time as possible to not only reach your exit goals but you identify what goals you are going after early on. There is an old Chinese proverb that states "A journey of a thousand miles begins with a single step." If your first years are spent traveling in the wrong direction because that first step sent you in that direction, you could end up spending years trying to find your way back to the path of your true thousand mile journey.

So why is it so crucial for you to read this book and start working on your business right now? The first factor of our equation above is *time*. This is the most obvious answer to that question. The sooner you get the process underway the more you can get done before that inevitable date comes. We will talk more about time later.

The other factor that you need to consider in why now is the time to start is that you are not alone. Baby boomers account for a vast majority of the small- and medium- size business owners out there. If you are one of these baby boomers you are well aware that you and many of your compatriots are nearing the age of retirement. That means that a great number of businesses will be hitting the market and looking to be sold. What makes your business stand out? What is going to cause multiple buyers to show interest in your business when there could be multiple similar situated businesses also being listed? It's not enough to just create a sellable business. You must find ways to go beyond that bare minimum and position your business in a way that stands apart from the crowd. That is why it's so important to create a business with the valuable characteristics a potential buyer is going to look for. The more of those value drivers, the more demand increases for your business and the more likely you are to have a successful transition out of the business. But you can't just flip a switch. These things take time to implement.

You can go to www.SellSmallBiz.com to find more information to help evaluate your own business. Find out what areas you are strong in and what areas you need to work on. This will give you an indication of just how much time it will take to get your business ready to be sold and let you know how you compare to other similar businesses to yours.

PART III

MISTAKE #2
EVERY BUSINESS CAN BE SOLD FOR SOMETHING

6 Driving the Value Bus

In trying to drive up the value of your business it is key to look at the acquisition through the eyes of the buyer. Creating stability, ease of transition and reducing potential risks are things that a buyer desires in an acquisition. Even if the buyer sees potential between their current operation and what your business can add to it, they still want to feel comfortable that your operations are going to perform and not hurt what they have.

The more stable you can make your business, the more processes that you can systematize, and the more risks you can eliminate or reduce, the more value that your potential buyers will see in your business.

Here is the easiest concept for most people to compare this idea to. One thing that many people are familiar with is buying and selling a home. I want you to take a minute and think about that process. When you were considering buying a home, I am sure you had a list of needs and wants for what you were looking for. Certainly, price and location were large factors, but there were other things you were looking for. Even if some houses met certain criteria, there may have been things you saw that were deal breakers. There was a reason you didn't put an offer on that one you looked at, remember?

When it comes to getting a home ready for sale there are certain things that are easier to clean up. A fresh coat of paint on the walls, fixing the loose banister and getting the carpets cleaned are relatively simple tasks. Then there are some middle of the road tasks that can add value. Things like redoing the landscaping in the front of the house, repainting the outside of the house and staging your house are steps that can drive up the value a little bit.

There are even things beyond that such as redoing the kitchen, installing new appliances or finishing your basement that have some major impacts on your home's value. These are things that increase how desirable your home is and entice more interested buyers which can drive up the ultimate purchase price.

There are also some negative elements that can really hurt how desirable your home is. Think about a crack in the foundation, a furnace that needs to be replaced, a roof that needs to be redone or hardwood floors or carpeting that has to be replaced. How awesome does a house have to be for you to pay the full value when a house has one these types of flaws?

Think about when you have looked at homes for sale. Were there any that you thought were close but had just one or two things that you couldn't live with? Or maybe you looked at one and the list of little things that had to be done were a turnoff? I bet there are some of you that have actually put in an offer below the asking price and based it on those "problems" with the house. I once made an offer on a house that was 10% below the asking price. The house would have been a great fit for my family but for the fact that it did not have central air. Was central air really worth a 10% reduction? Probably not but the fact was that if I wanted it, I would have to hire someone to install it. That was enough in my eyes to justify the request. By the way, we actually found another home that was just as good a fit with central air that we ended up purchasing and thank goodness we did. A couple of summers later when my wife was pregnant with our second child, the central air was working overtime to keep her comfortable.

Your business is very similar to your home. Interested buyers are almost looking for a reason to not buy. At a minimum, interested buyers are looking for "areas of concern" so that they can reduce the offer price. You have the ability, with some preparation, to fix those proverbial cracks in the foundation and, at the same time, maybe redo some of that landscaping too.

7 Optimization

Unlike a home, which is a tangible asset, your business is not as tangible. While you can "fix up" your home, "fix up" isn't really an accurate term when it comes to your business. Instead, you should think of more like optimizing your business because in reality that is what you are doing when you are working to create more value in your business. Yes, you are working on the business to try and make it more appealing to a potential buyer, but you very likely will see the results of your efforts pay off for you. In fact, you might have to make the decision whether you really want to sell because it's not uncommon when the business becomes optimized that the owner or owners suddenly are reenergized and want to see to what heights they can take their business.

Take a look at your marketing as an example. I am not going to be the guy to give you marketing tips. I do know that social media is not really free advertising, so there is your one tip. But let's say you work to get your marketing down pat. Your message, your branding, your advertising, your channels, your partners, and everything else about your marketing is running like a Swiss watch. Suddenly you are in a position that you can train someone else on how to run that marketing department, right? You might check in from time to time, but overall that area of the business is on cruise control because you have gotten it to a point that it's basically automated. Maybe a tweak here and an update there, but by optimizing the business' marketing you have worked yourself out of that job. Now what?

That is exactly what you want to do with everything you are a part of. Get to that point that you are able to ask: "Now what?" When you are moving on to other areas of the business or are working on growth strategies for the business, your position in the business completely changes. Suddenly you are the one pulling the strings and not the one getting pulled in a million directions. It is this position that many more buyers will be interested in, but you might be enjoying your ability to travel, or how you can focus on other ventures, or how much fun being a business owner who actually controls the business (as opposed to having the business control you), that you don't want to ride off into the sunset so fast.

The following chapters cover a few of the factors that can not only get your business to a point that it's a saleable asset but also drive up the value and attract interested buyers. At the end of each, take a moment and ask yourself: "How does improving in this area optimize my business?" Often it's rather obvious.

8 Management Team

Developing and deploying a management team is one of the toughest things for a small business owner. It can seem daunting to give up authority and control of the business that you have built from the ground up. Overcoming this hurdle can add incredible value to your business. Not only can a management team make your business much more efficient while you still own it, it can also help ensure stability for the new owner and make the transition much easier.

Many businesses run with the owner or owners acting as the only management. This means that you as the owner might have to oversee the operations, the marketing, the financial, the sales, the human resources and the customer services departments of your business. I am sure you are an incredible individual but if you are anything like me, you are not the best person to run all those different areas.

Not only are you likely not the best individual to run every one of those areas, but trying to manage all those areas takes you away from the areas you are great at. If you are like most business owners, you are really good at the operations aspect of your business. You are really good at the technical aspect of your business that actually delivers the product or service. Even if you spend only 20 hours a week on all the other aspects of your business other than the operations, that means you are going to have to work 60 hours per week just to get 40 hours in your optimal role.

Now I am sure that the marketing, the financial, the sales, the human resource and the customer service aspects of your business take up more than 20 hours of your week. I am also pretty confident that you are not a big fan of working over 12 hours per day or working on the weekends. Can you see the issues with your business if you are trying to act as the entire management team?

A great management team really has a twofold effect in driving the value of your business. First, no one is an expert at every job in a business. This means as you hire people who are able to fill roles that are not your strengths, those roles in the business are run that much more efficiently and that much more effectively. In other words, hiring the right management team can turn your weaknesses into your business' strengths. Second, you are able to free up your time to really focus on your strengths and the value you can add to the business. This includes your ability to work on the business as opposed to working in your business.

The more areas of your business that can be taken over by others, the less your business needs you. This can be a scary thought for some business owners who derive their own personal value on how much their business relies on them. At the same time, if you can put yourself in a position where you are managing your managers while they run your business, a buyer is going to be much more interested in your business.

A business with a strong management team holds tremendous value in the eyes of a buyer. A buyer is going to much prefer being able to come in and run a business as opposed to having to come in and either hire someone to manage a department or departments of your business or having to manage those departments themselves.

In addition a strong management team ensures that the business is going to have the ability to run much the same as it runs now after the transaction is complete. If your managers run their departments and remain on after the sale of the business, they can still run their departments. Thus there is continuity and the business will likely have little to no fall off.

Contrast this to where the management of those departments is taken over by the new owner or by a new hire of the new owner. If the new owner is managing a department or a new hire is managing a department of your business, there is a learning curve and potential they won't be able to match your abilities. Thus the business potentially might not be as valuable under the new owner.

In short, a strong, well developed management team not only allows your business to run much more efficiently now (and thus increase its value to you) but also makes it much more stable while reducing risk for a future owner (and thus increase its value to a potential buyer). Putting your ego aside and giving up having your fingers in everything that the business does can be a hurdle to overcome, but the value added can be immense.

9 Customer/Vendor Agreements

You have bad agreements and contracts on your books right now. There are two ways this statement is generally taken by a business owner. Either the owner asks which agreements might fall into that category or they vehemently deny that any of their agreements could be bad. The former group at least acknowledge that there might be issues lurking under the surface that they don't know about but the latter group is in denial.

To the latter group: I know that you had an attorney draft your standard language for you. That attorney was probably very qualified and maybe a little expensive. With each passing day though that language gets more and more stale. How long has it been that you have been using that language? Five years? Ten years? More? I am sure you have never had a problem with your agreement. Just because you have never had an issue with it does not mean that an issue won't arise. And good luck trying to convince a potential buyer that he won't have an issue with it either.

Vendor and customer agreements are the lifeblood of your business. Vendors bring in the supplies you need in order to function, while customers pay you for providing them with what they need. If the vendors go away, that can potentially shut your business down. If your customers stop buying goods and services, that can also shut you down. The agreements you put in place with those vendors and customers can make sure those relationships remain strong and dictate how any potential conflict would be resolved. You might want to rethink how confident you are in those agreements going forward.

Here is the good, the bad and the ugly of your customer and vendor contracts:

A. The Good: Change

No matter how long you have used the same agreement with a customer or a vendor, there are always ways to update that agreement. There is no hard and fast rule to live by when it comes to how to amend an agreement, but generally there is not an agreement out there that cannot be changed.

The easiest way to go about updating the agreement is to approach the other party and work out better terms that work for both parties. I once had a client who was working under the same pricing terms for the past 7 years. When we approached the customer about changing how much each unit cost, the customer actually admitted they wondered what took us so long to ask for the pricing to be changed. Could you possibly have customers out there that believe they should be paying you more? They are probably not going to chase you down to tell you that information.

If the other party refuses to negotiate new terms, there are very likely terms in the agreement that can give you leverage. Some agreements have provisions about how terms are updated and how those updates are made. Nearly every agreement has terms on how the agreement is terminated. In the worst case scenario, you have to wait for the term of the agreement to run out and then seek new terms with that customer or vender or you find a viable alternative.

The sooner you can get these changes in place the better. I have helped clients increase profits in years when their revenues dipped because we worked out better terms with vendors. In fact, when the market or the overall economy slows, is often the best time to try and get more favorable terms from a vendor. They are experiencing the same outside forces as you and want to keep you as a customer. These adjustments can add up a lot and when the revenues do increase, your bottom line looks that much better.

These changes to agreements do not even have to be completely monetary in nature either. Obviously with any business cash flow is vital. You want to receive payment sooner and want to pay bills as late as possible. Even if the amount of money being paid doesn't change, payment terms might be able to change. You can also get other "perks" added to the agreement. Things like special delivery terms, exclusivity and other similar type terms might not cost the other party anything to give you, but they can make a big difference in how your business runs. These are things you may be leaving on the table because you are using a standard agreement.

B. The Bad: Pain Isn't Always Noticeable

It is easy to avoid looking to update your customer and vendor agreements. The status quo is easy, especially if no one else is complaining and no major issues rear up. The pain to your business is not always noticeable though. You might be hurting your business by taking this easy path.

The most obvious pain is leaving money on the table. If you have been selling your widgets to Acme Corp. for 7 years at the same price but the cost of making widgets has increased 15% over those 7 years, that means you are not making the same profit on selling your widgets to Acme Corp. as you did when you first agreed to those terms. When was the last time you really dove into your numbers and made that assessment? When was the last time you increased your prices for your longest standing customers?

Even worse than the increased cost of making the widgets impacting your bottom line, is if you know that market rates have increased over the past 7 years. That not only means that you are not getting a fair market price for your product but your customer is very likely to know that he is getting a deal. In other words, if everyone else is selling widgets for $100 per unit and you are "stuck" in an agreement with Acme Corp. selling them for $85, don't you think Acme Corp. would agree to an increase as long as it remained below $100? They are still getting a deal from you, a trusted supplier for the past 7 years compared to if you just terminated the relationship and they have to go find a brand new supplier that is going to charge them the fair market rate. Are you keeping up with market rates? You can still be below market rate and increase your profits.

Other pain points that you don't notice are potential risk, potential litigation and potential loopholes. Businesses always have a tendency to evolve and so do their product offerings, their standard operating procedures and their relationships with vendors and customers. This evolution can mean that terms that once were accurate can now be inaccurate and represent potential issues for the business. These issues at best can present a way for someone to escape from their agreement with your business and at worst can end with a lengthy litigation process.

There are many examples of these issues creeping up. Too many to cover them all. But in order to give you an idea of how this can happen, here is one. Let's say you manufacture and sell a machine. One of the parts is produced by XYZ, Ltd. who states that they will guarantee that part for 10 years. When you draft your standard sales agreement with your customers you pass that warranty on to them stating you will warrant that part for 10 years. The problem is that was drafted 7 years ago and when XYZ, Ltd. sent you their revised agreement 3 years ago, you didn't really pay attention to the fact that they limited their warranty to only 5 years. Now because you haven't updated your standard sales agreement, you are potentially warranting that part for 5 years past when the vendor will guarantee it. What happens if the reason they ratcheted back the number of years was because they switched to a lower quality material and the part has an average lifetime of 7 years? You might be getting a lot of customers asking for you to pay for a new part very soon.

Buyers not only knock you down in purchase price because you are not maximizing income, but they reduce it more because of potential risk. Yes it is true that buyers will be interested in a business that they believe has the ability to increase its profits. At the same time, they are not going to provide you with an offer that is reflective of that potential and they might actually lower their offer because of the potential loss of business in correcting your mistakes. They also do not want to assume a lot of risk if your vendor and customer agreements have loopholes, potential risks and potential litigation. These are all pain points that you didn't even realize you had until the potential buyer brought them to your attention and that is not the person you want to point them out to you.

C. The Ugly: The Devil is in the Details

Contracts do not seem like a complicated thing to deal with. Most of the time these days contracts are drafted in a plain language style and much of the legalese is absent. It would seem that there is no need to hire an expert in this area. Offer, acceptance, written and signed, etc. It seems pretty straightforward.

I both agree and disagree with this notion. I agree that anyone who has worked with contracts previously can get most of the provisions of a contract down on paper regardless if that person is a contract attorney or not. Where the issues lie though are in the details of the contract. Eighty percent of a well drafted document still leaves a long way to go before you have a well drafted agreement.

Let's revisit our XYZ, Ltd. limited warranty situation above.

That is an easy detail to overlook. It's not like XYZ, Ltd. eliminated the warranty or significantly changed what situations they would warranty. All they did was change "ten" to "five." How many of us would have caught that? And how many that caught it would have put the pieces together to identify how that impacts other contracts?

It's also easy to overlook the importance of "standard language" in an agreement. Many contracts have general terms at their conclusion that govern how the contract will be governed and what parties can and can't do in regards to their duties under the provisions of the agreement. One common term is "Assignability." There is a big impact on you if that provision states you have the right to assign the benefits and responsibilities of the agreement to a third party versus a more standard version which prevents it. If you do not hold the exclusive right to assign the benefits and responsibilities under the agreement, how can you sell your business and assure that contact will be assigned to the buyer?

Retail business owners often tune out when it comes to contracts because "they don't use those in their industry." But retail businesses have important relationship details with both vendors and customers. Vendors often like to restrict how low you can advertise their goods for. You also might want to look at those terms and conditions on the order form you sign with your rep. You might be surprised at who is responsible for those goods even before they make it to your store.

Retail businesses also have a much higher volume of customers than other types of businesses. More customers means more potential disputes or lawsuits. What are the terms of your return policy? Are you properly disclaiming warranties? Are you limiting your liability? What happens if a customer is injured by a malfunctioning product they bought at your store and they name you as a responsible party?

Before you sit there and say, "Come on. I sell clothes. What is the worst that could happen?" remember that anyone can bring a lawsuit for anything. What happens if someone is wearing a shirt you sold and they get a little too close to an open flame and the shirt goes up in flames incredibly fast? Have you protected yourself enough?

The details of your contracts are extremely important and they are often the most overlooked aspect of contract development. Making sure that you have fully protected yourself, being sure your business is going to run as expected and confirming that the contracts work together for your overall goals, need to be a priority. The results add to the value of your business.

Overall contracts are so vital to any business. Making sure your contracts are working for you and not against you will add value to you as the current owner of the business. Less time dealing with disputes, better relationships and better terms will save you time and money. Great contracts are also going to drive up the value of your business in the eyes of everyone else. A potential buyer is going to want to not only feel confident that there are no potential issues but also feel confident that the business is protected as much as possible. Taking the time now to start implementing the changes and putting processes in place to regularly review and update the contracts your business uses can have a major impact on your business.

10 Employees

There is some crossover between employees and management team. Similar to why a strong management team is important, having a stable full of great employees can make your business even more profitable and require less of your time in doing day-to-day work in your business and supervision.

A business is really just a collection of employees. There are very few businesses out there that are so unique to the world that there is no competition. What makes Company A perform better than Company B? Maybe it's better products or services. Who is making those products, innovating those products, delivering those services, etc.? Maybe Company A has better sales people or better marketing. Again, who is doing the selling and marketing? Really, it comes back to Company A has a better team than Company B.

Acquiring, keeping and maintaining your employees can be a huge value driver. Not to beat a dead horse with this theme, but if your collection of employees makes you Company A, not only does that add value to you as the current owner of the business but that makes you stand apart when you are looking to sell your business too.

A. Employee Relationships

When we are talking about employee relationships, we are not talking about how you can walk the floor of your business and have a friendly conversation with any one of your employees or how you throw an annual holiday party in December to thank them for their hard work throughout the past year. While those things are important in ensuring your employee morale is high, the employee relationships we are talking about are a little more technical in nature.

There are three things that many business owners never institute that can add real value when it comes to a potential buyer's evaluation of their business. Many business owners never consider implementing employment agreements, employee handbooks or a human resources department.

Most states are considered "at-will" employment states. "At-will" employment is generally regarded as either party has the right to terminate the employment relationship at any time regardless if there is cause for such termination or not. This means that an employer can fire an employee at any time or an employee can quit at any time.

Because so many of us have employees that are "at-will" it can be tough to see why you would have an employment agreement with your employees. My thoughts on this are that "at-will" employment only governs the term and termination areas of the agreement between employee and employer. Many businesses have written agreements with customers that do not contain provisions about term and termination of the relationship. Often the termination of those customer agreements are defined by statute or other law so what makes an employee relationship any different?

In fact there might be even more of a reason to have employment agreements than customer agreements. Employment agreements allow you to ensure that each employee knows what jobs and duties they are to perform and how they will be compensated for those jobs and duties. You can also protect the intellectual property of your business and incorporate other agreements and policies into your employment agreement. In fact, if the proper notices are not provided to all employees, there may be certain Federal intellectual property statutes that can be unenforceable by you if your employees improperly use your trade secrets. It is also a lot easier to give constructive criticism or discipline an employee when you have an agreement where they stated they would do something and they are not doing it.

Employee handbooks fall into a similar vein as employment agreements. Unlike the employment agreements, which are drafted specifically for each employee, employee handbooks are general rules, policies and operations of your business. These rules, policies and operations are generally wide ranging but are very important.

If you believe one of your employees is using drugs and it's impacting his work, are you allowed to require that he take a drug screening? What is the dress code for your business? How many weeks do you allow new mothers to take for maternity leave? How many times can an employee be late to work before he gets in trouble? How are performance reviews and pay increases handled? How does the company handle a garnishment notice? What is the sexual harassment policy? The answer to these questions and more are all in a business' employee handbook. With rules, policies and operations in a codified form in the employee handbook, there is a much greater chance that you will maintain a better relationship with your employees because they know that everyone is being treated the same and they know how different situations are going to be handled right from the start of their employment.

Having good employment agreements and an employee handbook in place will also decrease your chances of having a disgruntled former employee bring a lawsuit against your business. If you have to terminate an employee because they breached a term in the employment agreement or one of the policies in the employee handbook, you are in a position of strength to defend against that former employee claiming they were terminated because of discriminatory practices.

The final layer of protection is to have a human resources department or HR department. This is not an area that you want to run on a discount. Even if you are a smaller company that doesn't need to have a fully staffed HR department, you can work with an independent contractor that can act as your HR department. There are lots of businesses out there that offer HR services and they can be a real asset.

Questions can abound when the number employees working for you grows. Do you know if you are compliant with the Affordable Care Act? If one of your employees believes you, the business owner, is harassing them, who can they report it to? If an employee gets sick and is absent for an extended period of time, do you have to wait for them to come back to work and then how long after they are back before you can terminate them? What information do you need to keep in an employee's file? Do you have to give the employee's file to them ever? These are all questions you may have thought of or that have kept you up at night. Your HR department will be an expert at these matters and able to quickly resolve issues as they inevitably arise.

Going back to your overall goal of wanting to create a valuable business, consider how a potential buyer would look at your business when it comes to employee relationships. Being able to show the terms of every employee's engagement with your business, the rules, policies and operations of the employees and being able to provide proof that you have great employee records and are in complete compliance with employment laws and regulations will go a long way to adding value. Not only can a potential buyer see the current state of your relationship with your employees but feel there is a relatively low risk of a potential compliance issue that will have to be dealt with. While these things might seem trivial or burdensome for you to implement, you can see how much a potential buyer would want to have them in place. Even more, what seem minor and inconvenient documents and systems to put in place can turn into potential life savers if a potential employment dispute arises.

B. Talent Acquisition

As I am writing this there is a severe talent shortage in the economy. There are actually some out there buying other businesses just to acquire the skilled labor they need. Your business may be like these businesses and you are currently looking for new employees to help you meet demand but you are finding it tough to find qualified candidates. This situation is not because you are not offering a desirable position or are not getting your call for applicants in the right location. It's because with unemployment rates so low, there are not many candidates that need a job.

This situation that we are currently in will likely not last forever. It does, however, exemplify a universal business need to employ talented employees. Whether the talent pool is full or empty, your business is only as good as the employees that work for it.

I think one of the greatest visuals of the need for talent can be seen in the US Olympic basketball team. In 1992 the US Olympic Team was comprised of the greatest basketball players in the world. Eleven of the twelve players on that team would go on to become Hall of Fame inductees, including Michael Jordan, who was in the peak of his career at the time. The team was loaded with talent. If you selected the top-10 professional basketball players of that era, you likely would have seen 8 or 9 of these guys on that list.

That team absolutely dominated. They won all 6 of the games they played in the Tournament of Americas to qualify for the Olympics by an average score of over 50 points. They won all 8 games they played in the Olympics by an average score of over 40 points. That Olympic run is more remembered for players of opposing teams asking for autographs, US players fighting to be the one to guard the opponents' best player and opponents asking for the US to take it easy on them than it was for anything else.

You compare that 1992 US Olympic Team to the 2012 US Olympic Team. While both teams won the gold medal, the 2012 US Olympic Team was not nearly as dominant. Even though the 2012 US Olympic Team is filled with very talented basketball players, including the best professional player of his era in LeBron James, because many of the best professional basketball players were from outside the United States, the talent gap has been closed.

Your business might not be in the industry of international athletics but this visualization shows two groups of talented people that accomplished the same task are not necessarily equal. Let's say you already had a basketball team and you were going to acquire one of those teams above to fill out your roster. Which team would you want to acquire? How much more would you pay for that team than the alternative?

You can see how much more effective and efficient a very talented team can be for you and your business. Sometimes that means you have to pay an employee more than an alternative choice but when the team is packed with talent the return on the investment can be well worth the additional cost. Employees are also seeking compensation in other forms. Many will forgo higher salaries in order to receive benefits, working for a socially conscious employer, having flexible schedules, being able to work from home, feeling like they have voice in the business decisions, stock or other ownership options, etc.

There's a psychological aspect to bringing A Players. A Players want to work with other A Players. That means they will hire and recruit other talented employees and those talented prospects will desire to work for you because you have a strong team. At the same time, a B Player is not going to hire or recruit an A Player because that is a threat to their position in the company so they will hire C Players or below. This might not even be a conscious decision. Why do you think that Google, Apple and the like are never struggling to find the best of the best?

When it comes to adding talent to your team, there is always the option to do nothing. That is what many small businesses decide to do when they have to fill a position of need. Either the owner feels they can cover that missing piece themselves or they ask other employees to come together to cover it up. The owner sees having to pay someone else as an expense and not as an investment. Stretching even the most talented employee or business owner is never going to have the same impact as adding another elite employee to fill a position in your business.

Going back to the 1992 US Olympic Team, what would have happened if instead of playing with 11 future Hall of Famers they decided to bring only 5 of them. I am sure that those 5 guys could have gotten a lot done, but would they have won the gold medal? Even if they did manage to win it all, I bet that team would not have been as dominant as it was. A full team is better than 80% of a full team. If you want your business to go beyond just surviving to the next month, the next quarter, or the next year, you want to work toward a full team of talented individuals.

You can also see why a potential buyer would put a premium on adding a highly talented group of employees to their already existing team. When they know they are already in need of talent and they see how incredible your team is, that becomes a point of desire for them in the purchasing process.

C. Key Employees

Key employees can become crucial pieces in a transaction. A key employee is someone who your business relies heavily or totally on for a certain important business function. A classic example of this is your lead salesman or saleswoman. Sales is something that is heavily based in relationships. Many of the best at sales are great at building and preserving their relationships with key customers. If your lead salesman has accounts that make up 30% or more of your business' revenue, what is your plan if that salesman leaves abruptly? Where do you think a potential buyer's mind is going to be at if that salesman could leave the day after closing?

There are two methods that are generally used to solve the key employee issue and drive up the value of your business. Either you lock in key employees or you eliminate key employees.

Locking in key employees is generally the first route that many business owners turn to. In the United States, there is a public policy that we are free to develop business relationships (or terminate business relationships) with whomever and whenever we want. The idea of creating a mechanism that indentures an employee to your business can fly in the face of that policy. Because of this, the methods for creating the "golden handcuffs" have a tendency to incentivize key employees to choose to stay.

Deferred compensation and bonus plans are very common. These plans can be very creative but the general gist of each is that if the employee chooses to remain at the company for so many years then the key employee will get certain guaranteed compensation for hitting those milestones. If the employee leaves before hitting those milestone dates, she gets no part of the payment.

Another way to lock in a key employee (or at least protect the buyer more) is to give a certain amount of ownership in the company to them before the transaction. Many states will allow for more stringent restrictive agreements such as non-compete agreements or non-solicitation agreements, when dealing with former owners of a business. Thus the new owner will know that the key employee cannot directly compete or take key relationships with him. A buyer can also request that the key employee with ownership in the company provides transition services as part of the sale of the business. If the key employee chooses not to fulfill that obligation, the purchase price of the sale might be adjusted accordingly. Thus the buyer is assured that the key employee will work for the buyer for so many months or years at a minimum or the buyer can setoff what was actually received compared to what he expected to receive.

There are other ways to lock in key employees with insurance, retirement plans, stock options and more. The important aspect you need to look at is that the plan you create will assure you that the key employee will sacrifice a lot more than just a salary if he or she chooses to leave.

A much better value driver than locking in your key employees is to eliminate them. Think about a McDonalds for minute. Forget that it's part of a chain or that it's a franchise. Think about the operations of that restaurant. Does it matter if any of the employees are 30-year veterans of the industry? Does it matter if any of the employees have long standing relationships with customers? If any employee was to leave in the middle of a shift, would sales drop even 5% for that week or month? There are no key employees at a McDonalds and a buyer is going to have confidence that after the sale, the business is going to remain consistent.

Eliminating key employees is easier said than done. The process takes time and careful differentiation of whether an employee is a key contributor or just a great employee. It also takes a lot of systematizing of your processes. When an employee's role is systematized, it becomes a lot easier to not only identify ideal candidates and to train a replacement on what to do in that role but also generate consistent outcomes in performance. Well-defined roles with well-defined objectives can allow you to measure what is working in your business and what is not.

A word of caution: You might not be able to eliminate all key employees so don't try to become McDonalds. You likely are a key employee and a large value driver is removing yourself from the operations of your business as discussed above. That likely means you need to put at least one or two key management employees in place. While systematizing can reduce how "key" these positions are, it likely cannot eliminate them altogether.

D. Hire Slow and Fire Fast

This last topic regarding employees is not something that an outside party is going to see and think that it adds value to your business. In fact they very well might not see it at all. The mentality of hiring slow and firing fast is something that adds value by making your business more efficient in its operations.

Hiring slow can be a bit confusing and it's probably an oversimplification of the concept. Hiring slow means not only do you take your time in evaluating the potential candidate but you also have well-defined ideal for the candidate that is going to fit with your business on every level and that you are not hiring out of desperation or need.

You can go on every job board or classified ad and see the generic job postings. Things like "4-year degree or comparative experience required" and "Must have strong oral and written communication skills" abound on the internet. My personal favorite is "Must be able to multi-task." Like there is a human being out there that can focus on two things at the same time and not have one of them (if not both) go incredibly poorly.

These postings exist in abundance because they work. Candidates send their resumes in by the boat load. You then have to sift through all of these and find the candidates that actually possess the skills that fit the job you are looking to fill. Then you interview a couple times and narrow the field down. Maybe you do another round of interviews and then settle on your new employee. If you rush this process, you potentially miss big caution signs in a candidate and find out when it's too late that you made a bad hire. Taking you time to really dig into candidates to make sure they are a great fit is important because even when they are a great fit, it doesn't always work out.

Knowing what you are looking for in a candidate goes beyond the skills and experience that candidate possesses. You need to know the culture of your business, where you see your business going, where that employee is going, what the work environment is like in your business and what type of environment that employee is coming from, etc. If you are taking on someone to do the bookkeeping but that position is going to grow into a more accounting and controller position as the business grows, do you think hiring someone who is going to school to be a nurse is a good hire even if he has 10 years of experience as a bookkeeper for a similar business to yours? What about if you run a very casual office where flip flops and ping pong tables abound but the candidate has a background working in a very formal corporate setting? Making sure that the candidate you hire is a good fit beyond just the skills they possess can mean the difference between a long-term employee and someone that burns out in less than 5 years.

When you are put in a position that you have to hire out of desperation or need, you limit the time you take in the hiring process. How many times have you heard about a fast growing company that struggles to scale up because of employee turnover? The growth they are having is great but they need someone making sales calls yesterday, so when someone comes close to having the right skills and shows interest in the job they are hired. It doesn't take long for that new hire or the business to get frustrated and then the position is open again and the cycle works its magic again.

It is not uncommon for businesses to always be hiring. Even if they don't have open positions they are in the process of interviewing candidates that might fit jobs in the future. This allows those businesses to do two things. They have a pool of ideal candidates to call on if a job opens up. Even if some of those candidates don't accept the job, a big enough pool will likely produce one. The other thing it does is it allows them to identify the next great employee. If a candidate comes to the table that is just too good to be true, you can make space for them. When you are "always hiring," time is never an issue. You can hire as slow as you want.

On the other side of the coin, many employers are very slow to terminate a relationship with an employee. For starters, firing an employee is never an easy process. But it goes beyond that because of the fear of having to find someone to replace that person. What if there is no one better out there, maybe you can train them to be better, maybe they need more support from others on the team, etc. These are all emotional decisions you are making.

You have carefully built your business with defined needs and roles that have to get filled. If one of those needs and roles is not getting fulfilled, is only getting partially fulfilled or is not being completed with any quality, it throws off the entire plan you have put in place. Your business can't afford to wait around for that aspect to catch up with what is needed so it can get up to full speed again. There is no guarantee that person will ever be up to the job and think of all the lost time and effort that you and other team members will endure while trying to support and provide additional training to that one spot.

Think about that for a second. An employee not pulling their weight has a double impact on your business. Not only is your business not running optimally but you are losing other resources to try and make up in that area. That is on top of the fact that you are compensating that person the same amount to not pull their weight as you would to someone that was doing a great job. This is why you need to be quick to cut the team members that are just not living up to expectations.

Overall your employees are like a garden of wild flowers. If you put the right seeds in the right environment, care for them and remove the weeds, you can have the biggest, most beautiful garden ever. But if you let even one of the aspects slip, that garden isn't going to be as bright as it can be. The more aspects you let slip the more chance that your garden will barely survive.

11 Litigation/Potential Litigation

No one wants to buy a lawsuit. I am sure that if you have ever had the distinct, displeasure of being a part of a lawsuit, you wish that someone would have paid you and taken that lawsuit with them. The problem is that no one really wants to assume a lawsuit and they certainly do not want to pay for it. Lawsuits are financially and emotionally draining.

Litigation is not an uncommon aspect of doing business. It was recently reported that Donald Trump, personally and through his various businesses, has been part of 3,500 lawsuits over the past few decades. While that may show an extreme willingness to get litigious, there are times where events can catch up to you. Eventually someone is going to push things too far or you are going to choose to do business with the wrong person. It happens and it has to be dealt with.

The cost of litigation is twofold. There is the financial aspect. Attorney fees add up quickly and the litigation process is so dictated by precedent and court rules that make it seem at times there is no end in sight for those fees to stop. This can put a real crimp in your business' finances. That is all capital that could be used to go to any number of value building activities.

The other aspect that many people fail to consider when it comes to litigation is the emotional toll it can take. Unknown outcomes. Frustrating decisions and rulings by the court. Endless paperwork and discovery requests. Even though you know you are 100% in the right, it can be daunting and eventually you just want it to be over.

LITIGATION/POTENTIAL LITIGATION

Many of the previously discussed topics can help eliminate potential disputes from arising. When the event does arise though, it can be well worth it to have a skilled counselor on your side. The problem that many business owners run into when a potential dispute arises and they get to the point where they think they need a lawyer is that they seek the counsel of a litigation attorney. There is nothing wrong with any attorney who makes their living purely on a litigation practice. The problem that arises is you are speaking to an attorney who makes his living by going to court. He is not likely looking to quash the issue before its gets to that level. In fact he might not even consider the potential options to avoid litigation because his idea of dispute resolution involves getting a judgment and not so much negotiating an outcome quickly.

Having an attorney who not only knows your business but likely advised you on the situation before it became an issue can be a great asset. That attorney can help navigate your business through this dispute to a resolution much quicker and for a much more reasonable price than litigation would be. Even though you might not receive the perfect outcome, getting it wrapped up months or even years earlier can be well worth the slight pain you feel in negotiating a settlement.

Resolving litigious situations and potential claims increases your business' value in two ways. The first is that it frees you up from the weight of that issue. The other is you are not convincing a potential buyer to take on your litigation or how they don't need to worry about a potential claim coming back on them after they close the deal with you.

As we have already covered, litigation is a burden on your business. Tens of thousands of dollars to attorneys and hours and hours of your and your employees' time wasted. Let's say that you only have to expend $5000 and one day of you time to litigate a matter. This is obviously a gross underestimate of the time and money involved in the process, but let's use those low figures. Think of the marketing that your business could do with $5000. How much new business and revenue would that equate to? Think about your time. Even if you are not a vital piece to your business, that is a vacation day that you could have had instead. Time is something you can't get more of so once you lose it to this dispute, it's gone. This is how these things can slow your business down even at a very minimal level. Imagine the costs for a dispute with $100,000 in attorney fees and a month or more of your total time.

We have also already discussed how no one wants to buy a lawsuit. In fact, potential buyers will not only negotiate you down on price if there is pending litigation but they will do the same if there is a potential claim out there that has not been resolved. These potential buyers will also require you to remain involved in the litigation process or that you will assume liability if the company is hit with a judgment as a result of the litigation.

These are all things you as a seller would like to avoid. You don't want the purchase price to be whittled down. You don't want to have to stick around after the sale. You don't want to be responsible for damages to the business. Doesn't it make much more sense to wrap these issues up?

Litigation is a pain in the butt. There is no way around it. Yes, there are disputes that are worth fighting for. For the most part though, a sensible resolution is in the best interest of all the parties and can help your business out tremendously in the long run.

12 Strategic Acquisition

Strategic acquisitions can be one of the most significant ways to boost your business' value if they are done correctly. At the core these business transactions seem pretty straightforward and simple. You go out and buy a business that helps your business to either enter into a new market, open up new distribution channels, develop new products to sell to your existing customers, strengthen your team or a combination of two or more of these.

So let's go out and buy someone, right? Not so fast. Going barreling into a transaction can quickly lose the "strategic" portion of your strategic acquisition. You need to put a lot of work in on the front side of a strategic acquisition to ensure that it does not cause you to lose value on the back side of the transaction.

A. Your Company

First and foremost, you should not be thinking about a strategic acquisition if your business is not rock solid. This does not mean you need to be a 9-figure revenue business with free cash just pouring out of the books. It does mean that you have to be in a strong financial position, that you have the time to oversee this transaction and that your business has a strong business model and knows who it is and where it wants to go.

If you are worried about how to make payroll next month, you are definitely not in a place where you should be looking to take on another entity. A strategic acquisition is not as smooth a process as it looks on paper. The transition of integrating two businesses into one can have an initial financial impact on both businesses. Having the financial positioning that can weather that transition period is vital. While a business struggling to make payroll is probably far from ready, making sure that you have some solid reserves and that working capital issues are not coming in the near future are things that you need to have a grasp on.

You and your management team also need to have the time to be a part of the integration process. Most transactions are not "plug and play" type deals. You don't sign on the dotted line and suddenly your business has a new division and is making an extra $5M on its bottom line.

If you and your management team are all working 60+ hour weeks on your existing business, you probably do not have the time that is required to make a strategic acquisition successful. Your sales manager has to train the existing sales team on new products or has to try to reorganize two sales teams into one. Think of the amount of effort that it takes to bring in one new sales associate. Now multiply that by the number of sales associates that you just brought on board through the acquisition. This is the same situation for you and every member of your management team and their respective divisions. This doesn't even take into account who is going to oversee the entire process, work to remove redundancies and ensure the newly acquired business is running efficiently.

Finally, you must have a strong grasp on who you are and where you are going. It is so easy to get caught up in the idea of the acquisition and what it can potentially bring to your business that you lose sight of what has made your business successful up until now. Making small sacrifices during your strategic acquisition to get the deal done or to make it work with your existing operations can drastically change things that would otherwise have a big impact on your business.

A strategic acquisition is supposed to be an add-on to your existing business. If you don't have a solid business model and a solid business plan that you are committed to, a strategic acquisition can influence your business and become more than just an add-on. It can take away from what has made your business effective up until now and actually cause you to regress. Many an acquisition has taken a turn south and it's important you ensure that any acquisition is a fit and won't have a negative effect on your business.

B. Core Objectives

The key to making a strategic acquisition work is developing core objectives you are looking for in an acquisition. Again, this isn't a deal that you try and just acquire another business that boosts revenue. Your business needs to have a strategic goal it is looking to accomplish by making this deal happen.

Let's say you have a business that your biggest segment of buyers is customers that have bought other products from you before. You have the distribution channels, the marketing, the customer base, etc. in place already. Really what you need is more products to sell to them to increase the lifetime value of each customer. It might take you years of development to create new products. Your core objective in a strategic acquisition is to acquire a business that has products all ready to be rebranded and sold to your existing customers.

By focusing on this core objective, you can narrow the potential pool of targets. Once you have identified your targets, you can really hone in on those aspects of the targets that meet your objectives to determine if those targets are viable to accomplishing your core objective.

Going back to our adding products example above, while one target might have better margins, a better sales team and better conversion rates on their website, they might not be the most desirable target for your needs than another business that has better and more diverse products.

Drilling down exactly to what your business needs and what will add value to your business is what makes a strategic acquisition strategic. Yes it would be nice to add products with better margins, more qualified sales associates and a high converting website. But under your business' leadership you can probably increase the margins, you already have sales associates that can sell to your markets and your website probably can increase the conversation rate of new products that are added. Those other things only increase the value of your business slightly, while the real diamond to your business is your core objective.

C. Access to Capital

There are lots of books out there and internet "business gurus" that love to push the idea of being able to buy a business with little to no money. I will be the first to admit that not only are those types of deals available, but I have worked on a few of them myself. At the same time, there is a reason why buyers in those situations are able to be so aggressive with pushing for post-closing payment terms. Generally that reason is the business that is being acquired isn't a great business.

Sometimes we can get so caught up in the idea of growing our business by any means necessary that we lose sight of our real end goal: grow the value of our business. As you have seen, growing value mostly revolves around creating a great business (which is why even if you are not looking to exit your business, preparing as if you are looking to sell can be of great benefit to your business). If you are working internally to create and build a great business, what do you think adding a new business to the mix is going to do when that business has been run very poorly prior to you acquiring it?

Now I am sure there are some of you that read that and think, "Hey, I can get a sweetheart of a deal on a strategic acquisition because not only do I get it for cheap and it adds to my existing business but by implementing my current business' great practices, that business is going to grow too. It's a real win-win-win."

I am not going to tell you that you can't find a diamond in the rough. I am also not going to doubt anyone's ability to turn a business around. How confident can you really be that the business that you identify as a potential fit, that you can get a "sweetheart of a deal" on and that has the ability to integrate into your operations quickly, is really a diamond? What if it ends up being just a rock? Turnaround projects are not quick endeavors generally. Financial issues with suppliers, product issues with customers, and operation issues with employees are just some of the big things that have to be worked through. If that takes you one to two years to get through (and that can sometimes be a conservative timetable for a turnaround) that can be a one to two year delay on you getting to where you want to be with your strategic acquisition.

How do you avoid your strategic acquisition delaying the growth of your business and get it to have a near immediate improvement on things? Make sure that the business you are acquiring is also a great business (or close to it). That likely will mean that you are going to have to forgo the "sweetheart deal" and find a deal that involves you paying a portion, if not a majority, of the purchase price before closing and that you run a significant amount of due diligence before executing any agreement. That means you need access to capital.

Having access to capital goes beyond your ability to acquire a stronger business that can propel your business' growth, it is also a sign of your current business' strength and stability. If your business does not have access to excess capital that you are already making tactical decision on, you probably should not be thinking about a strategic acquisition (See Section A of this chapter).

Stretching your finances too thin in trying to spur growth can backfire quickly. Instead your focus should be on growing your bottom line so you have access to extra capital.

The final reason why you want access to capital as part of a strategic acquisition is that there are always hidden costs when transitioning a new entity into your existing operations. Training, integrating, retooling, organizing, new system development and refinement are some of the many aspects of a strategic acquisition that can often be overlooked. Even if you are planning on eliminating redundancies between the two businesses, someone has to put the time in to review those redundancies, determine the best way to eliminate them and then integrate everything over from the other business. That takes time and effort. If you are the one that is overseeing that then what are you not doing in your current business while you are doing that? Does that cost you money?

Many businesses will hire an adviser or consultant that can assist with the transition process because it can be complicated. Even with expert help, there can be an adjustment period where revenue dips slightly. That is lost revenue.

Let's look at the simplest strategic acquisition: your business acquires another business simply for its lone product that you can manufacture and sell within your operations. Even in the situation where your facilities don't have to change anything to manufacture the new product and no efficiency is lost in training production and sales on the new product, at a bare minimum you need to increase your marketing budget in order to launch your new product to the public. Everyone knows you for other products so you need a major campaign to train your customers and markets that you now offer something new.

Now this strategic acquisition example is way oversimplified because even with the acquisition of a new product there are at least a half dozen other issues that cost your business time and money. Ensuring that you have access to capital to cover your business for these costs is important.

From this you might be thinking, "Who in the heck would ever get into a strategic acquisition if there are so many costs associated?" You are correct that a strategic acquisition is not something to go running into blindly. You have to take into careful consideration the return on the investment. If your business is currently doing five million dollars in revenue with 20% margins, it might be tough to see your business getting to ten million dollars in revenue and 25% margins in a couple of years organically. If you could acquire another business that could push your business to those numbers, what would you be willing to pay for that? Do you have access to capital to make that happen?

D. Homework

You have a strong grasp on the identity of your business, you know what the core objectives are in an acquisition, and you have access to capital. Now what? It's time to go to work.

You need to start by identifying your targets. This might start with searching the market for businesses that are for sale, but it can extend into businesses that are not being listed for sale. The perfect strategic acquisition partner may very well not have even thought about being bought up until you approach them about the possibility to be bought. Sometimes the best deals come from those that are not listed because you can create a prop deal (this is a deal where they are not listed and you are the only potential acquirer so you know that you are not bidding or negotiating against another potential buyer) or they are not prepared to be acquired and so the value drivers we are discussing are not in place for them. You have to do your research and really dig to identify those targets.

After you identify your targets and you narrow the list to who you are ready to go after, the real homework begins. This is where you start picking apart this business. You are the one trying to discover reasons why you should <u>not</u> buy this business. Once you go through that process and you really have tried to find a reason not to acquire the target, if the deal still looks good, you might have a strategic acquisition on your hands.

13 Last But Not Least

There are many other areas that you can work on in your business that raise its value. These ways are numerous and to go into detail on every one would take much longer than you probably care to read about. I would like to briefly touch on a few others to give you a bit of a taste.

A. Finances

Your finances provide a window into the lifeblood of your business. Buyers want to not only see "good numbers" but they want those numbers to be reliable. Many businesses make the mistake of not have very good books. This can be especially true for some of the best businesses because they are so cash rich that they don't need to be deadly accurate with the books. Even those great, cash rich businesses are going to get knocked down a peg or two if their books are unreliable. Financials that are audited can be a big value add because then the books are reflective of what is really happening.

One of the measurements that buyers like to see is cash flow. Some like to say that cash flow is king. The general rule that everyone knows (but many ignore) is you want to get paid sooner and you want to pay later. Do you operate your business in a manner that requires customers to pay you upfront for goods or services? Do you have to pay vendors after 30 days? 90 days? Those little things that create a more positive cash flow cycle can be attractive to buyers.

In the same line of thinking, if your business is able to fund itself buyers will be more attracted. If a business does not need to rely on a bank for a line of credit or loans in order to finance its operations, that saves the buyer from paying interest in addition to opening up the credit that is available to the buyer to be put toward growing the business and not funding operations.

Finally profit margins are important too. Not only can improving profit margins put more money in your pocket as the owner, the higher the margins you have the more interest is going be piqued in buyers. Even more enticing is if your business' profit margins can increase with the number of customers. In other words, if a buyer takes over with the plan of increasing the number of customers your business services, if that alone would improve the profit margins, your business becomes more desirable.

These financial improvements can be daunting and take time to implement, but one step at a time and by the time you plan on exiting your business, they can add up.

B. Industry

The industry you are in can sometimes seem like something that is outside your control. At the same time, you can look at the industry you are in and see potential trends that exist or that are coming and maneuver your business to either strengthen its foothold in the industry or pivot to an industry that has better trends.

Obviously businesses that are in shrinking industries are not nearly as desirable as those that are in growing industries. Once you identify what trend your industry is on, your business' room for growth comes into play. Looking at whether your business can handle a spike in demand, asking how much of the market your business has infiltrated and determining whether there are edge products and services that can be added to your offering are all important.

If your business is thriving but production is not being pushed anywhere near its limits, there are lots of areas in a growing industry that you have not touched yet and if your product offering is limited, a buyer can see a ton of potential to grow beyond where your thriving business is right now. That potential is value.

C. Recurring Revenue

I cannot emphasize too strongly the importance of recurring revenue. Working to develop a business model where even a portion of the revenue is attributed to customers on some kind of automatic payment plan or subscription plan can not only improve your business operations while you are the owner, but that steady flow of revenue is very desirable to a buyer.

Recurring revenue allows you to have a more predictable income stream for your business. This allows you to budget much more effectively and cut out waste. Thus your business runs much more efficiently.

Also, because your customers are regularly receiving products and services from you, you remain preeminent when new needs arise that your products or services can meet. These recurring models are almost like free marketing by just delivering your products and services. Your team members are able to stay in contact with customers regularly and that helps them identify customer needs that you can fill or trends in the market that you could easily fill with a new product or service.

Buyers love predictability when acquiring a business. Remember most buyers view the acquisition as an investment. They are buying your business and they want a return for that purchase price. Predictable revenue means there is a more reliable timetable for the return on the investment.

D. Customer Service

Customer service is something that is extremely lacking today. It is something that everyone claims they are great at, but when you really look at your own experiences as a consumer, how many times are you really blown away by the level of service?

I am not even talking about when you have to call your bank and get put through the gauntlet of computerized prompts only to get transferred to a remote call center that may or may not be able to help you. That is bad but think about when you have last gone to a retail store or restaurant. Did you feel like you were a priority or did it feel like getting you in and out quickly was the priority? What about when working with one of your suppliers? Did you feel like you were the most important person they had to deal with that day or was it just an ok experience? Is your business really creating raving fans that go out of their way to recommend your business? That is what you want.

Many companies are switching from traditional customer satisfaction surveys to a net promoter score. The net promoter system is based on one question: On a scale of 0 to 10, how likely is it that you would recommend our company/product/service to a friend or colleague? Those giving a 9 or 10 are promoters of the business and very likely to recommend it. Those giving a 6 or under are detractors. These scores are starting to be used more when selling businesses because there is such an appeal to buyers for a business with truly great customer service and relationships. It is becoming a signal to a buyer that your customer base is more likely to exhibit value-creating behaviors, such as buying more, remaining customers for longer, and making more positive referrals to other potential customers.

Is your customer service really on the level that it draws out more 9's and 10's? Or is it just ok where you are getting 7's and 8's, which are considered neutral responses? This matters because it can lead to more revenue while you own the business, but it can be a huge selling point to a buyer.

14 Value Conclusion

This is far short of everything that would be considered a value driver for your business, but it hits on some of the bigger concepts. These strategic improvements to your business can change your business from being unsellable to sellable to extremely sellable. In fact, if executed properly, I would not be surprised if you chose not to sell your business immediately.

Close your eyes and imagine the ability to take one month or longer vacations and when you are in the office you are able to pick and choose what you work on. Think about how fun it becomes when you are doing your annual planning and you are allocating funds and moving pieces around like a chess master. Imagine the worry of invoices or payroll no longer being an issue.

This is seriously a possibility for your business. Your management team running the day-to-day operations not only allows you to leave for extended time periods and performance remains consistent but that allows you to have a much more flexible and strategic role in the business. Having great employees, strong customer relationships and awesome cash flow allows your business to not only thrive but gives you the stability to predict what's happening. And when you finally come to the decision that it's time to sell, you have to sell or someone approaches you about buying you out, you are in a position of strength to get the best value out of your business.

You probably want to know where your business is right now on the spectrum between unsellable all the way to your dream situation. Go to www.SellSmallBiz.com and take the free business evaluation there. You will get feedback on where your business stands and what you need to work on. You might be closer than you think to being ready to sell but you will never know until you take the test. If you know you are not ready to sell the evaluation is an excellent tool for benchmarking where you are at and coming up with a real plan on turning your business into a sellable asset.

PART IV

MISTAKE #3

YOU DON'T HAVE TO KNOW ABOUT THE STRUCTURE OF A DEAL UNTIL IT'S TIME TO SELL

Most business owners will only sell one business in their life and there is a good chance that one transaction will be the largest transaction they are ever part of. Because this is such a rarity it's good to get an overview of exactly what you are getting into when you want to sell your business. This scouting report will let you see the angles better, understand what we are getting ready for and why we do what we do.

This should go without saying, but a deal for a $500,000 company to a family member is quite a bit different than the sale of a $50,000,000 company to a publically traded company. Without going into a great deal of detail, let's just work under the assumption that some deals are more complex than others.

With the above assumption in mind, generally a deal starts off with an expression of interest, followed by the exchange of some high level information and then a letter of interest is executed. Once the letter of interest is put in place, a deep dive into your business or due diligence is done. After due diligence is completed there may be some further negotiations over the terms in the letter of intent based on what was discovered during due diligence. Then a purchase agreement is drafted and agreed to. Even after the deal is closed there are still post-closing obligations that must be met.

Is this process overwhelming to someone that has not been through it before? Absolutely. It can even be overwhelming to business owners who have been through it before, but at least they have some experience and have some knowledge of the process. Being prepared for what this entire process entails is important so you can limit this overwhelming feeling.

Let's break down each one of these steps so that you have a better idea of what is involved in a deal.

15 Expression of Interest

Getting to the expression of interest or EOI is the tough part of this step. An EOI is when potential buyers express interest in buying your business. The EOI itself is not complex, but what is necessary to get one or more potential buyers to that point takes work.

Generally if you work with an M&A broker or an investment banker they will market your business for sale through teasers. This teaser is basically an advertisement for your business that keeps your business' identity confidential but provides those that see it with information such as industry, revenue, growth potential, geographic area, maybe some generic information about your customer base and other similar type information. This information is meant to entice those that might be interested to hear more about your business and reach out.

A broker or investment banker should also help to put together a target list to receive this teaser information. This list will be comprised of potential buyers that meet certain criteria that you have set for what your goals of the sale to be. This can limit potential buyers to strategic buyers or to financial buyers. It can exclude competitors also. The list should help the teaser be more targeted because information can be formatted to hit potential buttons that are common among the members of this list.

Some brokers or investment bankers will list teaser information on websites that list businesses for sale. These websites have a similar look and feel to a real estate listing website, with the major exception that your business is not specifically identified like the address of a house might be.

EXPRESSION OF INTEREST

Regardless of whether a potential buyer comes out of the blue, through the marketing efforts of a broker or investment banker, or through the efforts of the business owner, once that potential buyer (or buyers) is there and has shown they are interested in taking a look at your business, there is the expression of interest.

Occasionally this EOI is formally put into an agreement, but more commonly it simply is shown by the potential buyer or buyers executing a non-disclosure agreement or NDA. This NDA will allow you or your representatives to provide the buyers with more detailed information about your business so that they can gage if they want to put an offer in to buy your business and what that offer would be.

I should caution you at this time that while NDAs are very useful tools when they are appropriately drafted, they are never full proof. You should always be cautious with the disclosure of confidential information. This does not mean that you keep everything under lock and key, but if a potential buyer is a competitor of yours and would like a tour of your facility, you may want to go as far as covering up proprietary equipment. A certain level of common sense needs to be used. Reveal too little or vague information and none of the potential buyers will give you an offer. Reveal too much and you risk giving away your proprietary information. I would recommend consulting with your advisers on what is too much information. There is a happy medium between giving away all your secrets and being too tight-lipped so that the potential buyers don't have a clue why your business is so great.

16 Letter of Intent

Once the EOI has been given, the next step is for the potential buyer or buyers to give you an offer. This offer is often given through what is known as a letter of intent or LOI. Basically an LOI describes the basic structure of the deal and how the transaction will proceed going forward.

Based on the information that was provided in the EOI step of the deal, potential buyers put together an outline that they believe is fair. This will include what type of deal they are willing to do, what they are willing to pay, how they will pay and any other requirements they may have as part of the transaction.

The seller has the opportunity to counter these proposed terms. This is why it is such a great benefit for a seller to have more than one potential buyer. If there are multiple offers on the table, not only are those offers driven up because there is competition to acquire your business, but terms that you find appealing in one offer that might not appear in the offer you believe to be the best fit for your business can be used as negotiating points to get a better deal.

These terms of the sale are not binding. Basically from a legal perspective, these terms of the LOI are just an agreement to make an agreement in the future. We will revisit this point in the due diligence section of the book because it is important to understand what impact this fact has on you.

Even though the deal terms might not be binding, that does not mean that all the terms of the LOI are non-binding. Often the LOI will have other terms that involve how the transaction will go moving forward. These terms include how long and how due diligence will go for, which party will be responsible for drafting the purchase agreement, when the deal must close by, reincorporation of the NDA terms that were agreed to in the EOI and other similar terms. These provisions do become enforceable once the LOI is executed.

The other thing that many sellers inquire about is getting a down payment. Because the deal terms in the LOI are not enforceable, the potential buyer has the ability to walk away at any time from the deal. This means that as a seller you have invested time, energy and money in trying to come to an agreement with this potential buyer, while ignoring other potential buyers, for a sale that will never come to fruition. As a seller you might be saying, "Hey wouldn't it be nice if the buyer put a chunk of change down with the LOI so I could limit my risk?"

These types of down payments or security deposits do exist in some deals but that does not mean they are commonplace. The most common situation that you, as the seller, will have leverage to request such a payment is if there are multiple potential buyers giving you offers and the buyer wants you to exclusively deal with them and take the business off the market.

Even if you have that type of a situation and the buyer is willing to pay the down payment, there are specific restrictions on that down payment. To begin with, generally it will be credited toward the purchase price of the business at closing. It will also likely be held in escrow and not in your possession until that time. There will also be specific situations when the down payment will be returned to the buyer and other specific situations that it will go to you. While this type of a provision provides you with the security that the buyer is serious about buying your business, it is not a guarantee of anything more than that.

Once the terms of the LOI are agreeable to both you and the buyer, the document is dated and signed. This is a point in the transaction where a buyer and seller without the aid of advisers can get a little lost. The biggest killer of any deal is when the deal loses momentum and nothing is happening. Sitting around wondering what we do now should be avoided at all costs.

17 Don't Get Married To the Wrong Buyer

Before we get too far down the path of our transaction, let's touch on one topic that can sometimes get pushed to the side in all the excitement. You have been marketing your business for sale and have some interest from a few sources. Do you know who they are? What their plans are? Heck, why should you care? They are going to pay you a boat load of money for what you worked your butt off to build. What does it matter to you?

You really need to take into account what you want for your business. Maybe you are of the ilk that you do not care what happens after you leave your business. There are many other owners that care not only about the business they built surviving their lifetime but also about making sure that the employees that have provided so much for the owner are in a stable situation.

The wrong buyer can run your business into the ground. Or dismantle and sell it off piece by piece. Obviously if you were hoping for your business to be around for decades and for it to be a pillar in the community, if the next owner puts it out of business, by choice or circumstance, that goal isn't going to be met.

If the business you sold goes out of business, that means that all the employees that you spent working side-by-side with are suddenly looking for jobs. You might have gotten your retirement but many of your employees have years of employment still ahead of them before they can retire. If your business goes under after the sale, that can leave them in a position to be searching for new employment and we all know how tough that can be.

What is an even bigger issue to you, is if the deal you strike with a buyer has post-closing payments (i.e. the buyer does not pay the entire purchase price in cash at the time of closing), a buyer that cannot successfully run your business will likely default on making the required payments to you. That means you are not getting the full benefit of the bargain and either you are going to get shorted on the purchase price or you might have to take over the reins of the business again.

Before you jump on me and think that it's not common that a previous leader of a business is forced to get back involved, look at two massive companies, Dell and Apple. Both Michael Dell and Steve Jobs left their positions as CEO of their respective companies only to have to be called back into action when those companies struggled under the new leadership. I think we can assume the leadership that took over for those two was very qualified, but it shows that even well thought out choices can be the wrong choices.

Vetting out the best buyer of your business might be more than who can make the biggest offer. You might want to take a long hard look into what the buyers' qualifications are, whether they are a good fit with your business and what their long term vision for your business is after the sale. Your best option might not be based on a dollar figure on a piece of paper.

18 Due Diligence

Due diligence is often one of the most overlooked portions of the deal process by sellers. Whether they believe that the buyer is the one that has to do all of the work or that process will be easy or that they have nothing to hide, this is an area that the seller does not put much of an effort into preparing for. Let this be a fair warning to any seller, due diligence should be seen as one of the most important aspects of the deal, if not the most important.

Due diligence is when the buyer has the opportunity to really dig into everything about your business. In the car buying process this would be comparable to taking the car to your mechanic to check it out or in the home buying process this would be comparable to having the home inspection done. The difference between selling a business and selling a car or a home is that due diligence can feel much more invasive especially if you are not prepared for it.

Let's take a quick step back from your role as a seller and look at this deal through the eyes of the buyer. The buyer is about to take on a large investment in acquiring your business. Even if the buyer is a $100 million company and the price for your business is only a $1 million, the buyer is still going to want a return on that investment and want to ensure this acquisition doesn't cause more trouble than it's worth. Putting yourself if the position of a buyer, knowing the importance of making sure you get this right, don't you think when you have the opportunity to break down every aspect of the business from sales to operations to financials to management to everything else, you are going to capitalize as much as possible on that opportunity? Of course you are.

Buyers and their advisers and representatives are generally very cordial throughout the due diligence process, but they are looking to tear your business apart. They want to not only see exactly how your business ticks, but they want to nail down every possible risk that exists or potentially could arise in the future of your business. Needless to say, for the seller, this process can feel more like an interrogation than a genial conversation.

If you recall from our discussion that the deal terms of the LOI are not enforceable, this is where that fact is important. It is not uncommon for a buyer to want to reopen negotiations based on what they find during due diligence. Remember the purchase price is based on the money your business makes and the risks to that income. As the number of risks increases because the buyer discovers them during due diligence, the less the buyer is going to want to pay you for the business. The alternative to lowering the purchase price is the buyer being able to negotiate to pay more of the purchase price after closing, which we will delve into later.

Knowing that the due diligence process is so invasive and holds such importance to ensuring that you get the best deal possible for your business is half the battle. The other half is how to use that information to your benefit.

It is becoming more and more commonplace for business owners to actually run sell-side diligence. This is a process where you actually run diligence on your own business and prepare everything and anything that might be requested by a potential buyer. This allows you to not only deep dive into your own preparedness for sale but also gives you a high level of preparedness for the diligence process. When you have gone through the process, generally, the letter of intent is a more accurate representation of where the purchase price will end up at and you can basically hand over diligence to the buyer proving that there are no surprises.

19 Purchase Agreement

Once diligence is complete and final negotiations are hammered out, it is time to develop what will become the controlling document for the deal: the purchase agreement.

To call this a document can be a bit of an understatement. Even in simple deals the purchase agreement can easily extend to 20 pages. Often times there are supplemental agreements and schedules that accompany the main purchase agreement. Some of the supplemental agreements might include a lease agreement or real estate purchase agreement, a promissory note, a security agreement, a guaranty, employment or independent contractor agreements, non-compete agreements, an assignment and assumption agreement, bill of sale and other similar supplemental agreements. It is not uncommon for the purchase agreement with all the schedules and exhibits to extend beyond 50 pages.

Deals come in one of two flavors: an asset purchase or a stock purchase. Asset purchases are much more common. There are entire books and seminars dedicated to covering the difference between an asset sale and a stock sale. While it's probably not necessary for you to know all of the differences and intricacies (there is a reason you should hire an attorney), it is good to have some general knowledge of the difference.

An asset sale is a transaction where the buyer is going to acquire all of the assets of the seller. This includes all the tangible assets (equipment, inventory, raw materials, etc.) and intangible assets (intellectual property including the business name, customer relationships, employees, etc.). This type of transaction allows the buyer to acquire the business without having to step into the shoes of the seller and take on any unnecessary liabilities or risks. The biggest negatives to an asset sale are certain things can be difficult to transfer and as a seller you still remain liable for those risks the buyer isn't assuming.

A stock sale is a transaction where the buyer purchases all of the issued shares of a company and assumes control of all the unissued shares as well. Basically the buyer steps into the shoes of the seller. Buyers want to limit the amount of liabilities they assume in taking over, so they are naturally adverse to stock sales, whereas a seller would prefer a stock sale from the aspect that after the transaction is complete they can walk away.

There are many other differences in both these processes and neither is definitively better than the other all the time. When you start to factor in the tax implications to both the buyer and seller depending on if it is an asset sale or a stock sale, it will quickly become apparent that each deal is unique in which type of transaction should occur.

One other limiting factor to which type of transaction you pursue is if you use an M&A broker. Even though federal regulation has become more lax over the past few years, unlicensed brokers may not be permitted to conduct a stock sale under certain conditions. This means that many brokers only list asset transactions.

The purchase agreement step might seem like a formality. At this point, the seller wants to sell and the buyer wants to buy. The terms have been negotiated and the type of transaction has been decided on. All that needs to be done is the attorneys need to put everything down on paper, right? You would think so, but this is where the gory details come into play and we know who loves quibbling over the gory details: attorneys.

Most attorneys are not transactional attorneys. Even among those that have done a transaction in their career, many are not transactional attorneys. Even among those that do transactions on a regular basis and call themselves transactional attorneys, there are still some that are incredibly good at getting in the way of business getting done.

You need an attorney. No way around that fact. Going into and completing a transaction on your own is lunacy and asking for issues. Think of it from this perspective: there are businesses out there that make money on buying and selling businesses. These businesses conduct dozens of deals over the years. All of these businesses use attorneys in their transactions. They don't hire these attorneys because they are not experienced in conducting a transaction. They don't hire them because they have money to burn (most them report to investors so they are pinching pennies). Why would these experienced businesses that are not looking to waste money always use an attorney on a transaction? It is because they know that a great transactional attorney can make the difference between a successful deal and one that ends up becoming someone's "horror story" that gets told over and over again. If these businesses, with so much more experience with transactions than you, require that their attorney is involved, what makes you think that you are ok not hiring an attorney?

The next question you should be asking is "Who is a good transactional attorney that I can hire?" If you are thinking about the attorney that set up your business, the one that handled that collections suit for you or the one that represented your brother in his divorce, please refrain from hiring any of them. I am not going to say with certainty that these attorneys cannot handle your transaction and they very well might be very qualified to do so. But remember what we talked about above, even among those that are actually transaction attorneys, there are still some that are not a good fit.

When looking for the attorney to represent you in your deal you want someone who not only understands transactions but understands your business and your goals. Most attorneys are trained to be risk averse and impose their opinions onto others. This can be a bad cocktail of traits when trying to come to an agreement in a deal.

Let's take a quick look at a hypothetical. A common detail in a transaction that involves a promissory note is a clause that limits the buyer's ability to transfer ownership of the business, sell off assets of the business or materially change the business until the note is paid off. An attorney that is risk averse is not only likely to want to make this clause incredibly restrictive in order to protect their client but they are not going to listen to reason on why that clause needs to be taken down a notch. Rather they are going to try and impose their will on the buyer. Of course it is an attorney's job to protect their clients but, at a certain point, that protection gets in the way of the deal. Do you want an attorney who is going to stop or delay a deal because he feels the terms of the non-compete agreement are too broad when you have no problem with them?

A good transactional attorney will assess the buyers concerns with the clause and negotiate a solution. Let's say the buyer wants to buy another entity in the next 12 months and merge it with your business. There are all kinds of potential solutions that can be derived that allow this to be permitted but still allow comparable protection to the seller.

As you can see there is a clear difference between the mentalities of attorneys and it should be clear to you which one gets in the way of a transaction being completed and which one helps push the deal forward. Ultimately the decision of what is agreed to should be up to the client. A good transactional attorney will advise their client of the risks, provide some potential solutions and allow the client to decide how to proceed. Unfortunately, many attorneys tell their client what to do and it causes more issues and can sometimes kill a deal.

Having the right attorney as your adviser can make this purchase agreement step go a lot smoother than having an attorney that gets in the way of the transaction or even worse, doesn't know what they are doing.

Once all the back and forth comes to a conclusion, there is a main purchase agreement, between five and a dozen supporting agreements and a whole bunch of schedules. You can see how these documents can grow and be confusing if you are not used to building them.

Then it's time to close the deal. This is really just delivering the signed documents, making the payment and handing over the keys (figuratively at least). This is the moment that you imagine in your mind, sitting in some fancy boardroom, champagne on ice and everyone is ready to slap everyone else on the back in congratulations. While formal closings are not rare, what with technology and efficiency, closings are not necessarily filled with such pomp and circumstance. A scanned or faxed copy of the documents, a wire transfer and phone call is all that is really required. The closing generally falls somewhere in between these scenarios but it should be an exciting moment for all those involved.

20 Post Closing

Even after you have found a buyer, negotiated the price of your business, had that buyer go over everything about your business and even signed the purchase agreement, you have still not crossed the finish line. There is still one last step that needs to be completed.

There are an elite few business owners that get to closing and are able to ride off into the sunset. For a large number of owners, there are post-closing obligations that both the buyer and seller must complete. As a seller, you want to reduce these post-closing obligations as much as possible. A buyer wants to extend these out as much as possible because that means less cash exchanged at closing and more opportunity to reduce the purchase price.

A post-closing obligation is the actions and payments that are required to take place after the deal has been closed. Common aspects of the deal like promissory notes, transition services agreements, earnouts, and leases create these obligations.

A promissory note might not seem like that big of a deal if you are the seller. I mean all you have to do is wait for the buyer to pay you, right? I will ask you this: what happens if the buyer isn't able to step into your shoes and the business goes under? If that happens, you are probably not getting what you thought you would as part of the transaction.

The other thing that needs to be considered is what happens if the buyer feels you breached the purchase agreement by failing to disclose a liability, inflating financials or some other aspect of the business not being what was represented? Rarely does a seller actively hide these types of issues, but it's not uncommon for mistakes to get made during the chaos of the transaction. If this happens, the buyer is going to look to offset her loses against what is left to be paid after closing. That means that you have to choose if you want to dispute the discrepancy, negotiate a settlement or just rollover on it and accept it.

Many transactions are not actually complete for 3-5 years after the purchase agreement is signed. Potential reductions to purchase price and unwinding of the deal are always a possibility and the more time that those potential issues linger the more chance they impact you.

You are very likely never going to eliminate post-closing obligations from your deal unless it is a small deal. Just like how you are looking for security at the beginning of the deal, a buyer is going to want security that if there is a reason to reduce the purchase price they are not going to have pursue you to give some of the purchase price back. You very likely are not going to voluntarily return a portion of the purchase price. There are ways to reduce the number of post-closing obligations that your deal has. There are also ways to reduce the number of months that these requirements can impact you.

You can see why it can be incredibly important to not only create stability in your business for the transition to a new owner but how choosing the wrong buyer can impact you too. A great business that can survive without much input from you and a great buyer, can make the post-closing time of the transaction much easier.

PART V

MISTAKE #4

YOU HAVE IT MADE IN THE SHADE AFTER YOU SELL YOUR BUSINESS

There is one area that many a business owner has overlooked. What happens after?

Let's put you into a time machine. You have worked hard to develop your business to this point. Let's flash forward years into the future. After reading this book you started making serious changes in your business and getting it ready for sale. You have worked your butt off to essentially work yourself out of a job. Your business has flourished under this new philosophy and you closed a sale that was beyond your wildest dreams. And even though you worked the last 12 months (although in a very limited capacity) in assisting the new owner to take over, you could not have asked for a better deal to be struck. Now the ride is over. As the bartender's say at closing time, you don't have to go home but you can't stay here. So what are you going to do?

This is a topic that is rarely, if ever, broached by advisers. They see themselves in a position to help guide you through the process. Heck, some selfishly will forget about you after the transaction is done because you are no longer a source of revenue for them. Why would they give two hoots about what you are doing after?

This is something that any business owner has to carefully look into and consider. There are two major aspects to this:

1) the need to be needed and

2) personal fiscal planning

21 The Need to Be Needed

Let's be honest with ourselves for a second and consider the ego we are developing as business owners. We come into work on a daily basis and everyone looks to us as the leader. We are the ones signing off on everything that happens. We are the ones setting the priorities, strategies and values of the business. We are responsible for all those employees' jobs. We are the one that is making the impact on the community. When politicians jump on television and talk about how small businesses are the drivers of the economy, we know they are thinking of us. We are needed. Big time.

But after the sale of the business, that quickly changes. Suddenly the emails slow down. No one is calling you to ask your advice. You have nowhere to go when you wake up in the morning. You have no overarching goal to drive for. You don't even have a breakroom to head to where you can talk to others about last night's episode of whatever hot show is on television.

Now I know reading this, you are probably thinking that I am crazy. Who doesn't want to find the pot of gold at the end of the rainbow and retire off into the sunset? You are going to travel, right? You are going to build that perfect retirement house on the lake and actually be able to enjoy it, right? You are going to finally enjoy time with your family, right? And who doesn't secretly get angry when a phone call interrupts what they are doing or get fed up with the endless stream of emails? Heck, you might be able to get away from Chris' (that guy from Accounting) constant need to talk about the Detroit Lions and how this next year is going to be when they "restore the roar."

While all these things and more might seem like amazing distractions and pet peeves that you can finally escape from, remember that ego thing we talked about earlier? Yeah the need to be needed will catch up with many of us. The world will eventually slow down. There are only so many places to travel to or tasks that you can focus on. Then you will have to look yourself in the mirror and come to the reality of what is.

Make sure you have a plan for after the plan. Whether that is being a part-time consultant, investing in other ventures or maybe starting another business (you know that hobby business that you always thought would be awesome but never saw it as profitable as the one you are running now). I am no psychologist and I am not good enough to identify what you will need in this future (maybe by that time I will have started my own second act where I am helping with that transition), but I can tell you there are more than a few stories I have heard where a business owner gets everything they wanted and more only to realize they don't know what to do after attaining that peak.

22 Personal Fiscal Responsibility

I am not a financial planner or adviser. You will not catch me trying to give you stock tips or tell you where or when to spend your money. But what I do know is many business owners do not take this aspect into account when they exit their business and they are planning their big escape from the "real world."

Many business owners, especially those in high performing businesses, are very fiscally responsible. They have a set plan on what they are going to spend and what revenue and resources they have available. Many even have reserves on hand so they can operate for a time period "even if one red cent doesn't come in during that time." It seems odd that this jump doesn't get made to the personal side of things for a business owner.

Many business owners bank on the sale of their business for their retirement. There is nothing wrong with that, but if you are not discussing and planning for what you need to retire then you might not be able to retire from the income you get from the sale of your business. Heck, you might not even think of everything that will impact that purchase price after you receive it. Suddenly the $5,000,000 purchase price is reduced by taxes, and you are celebrating by buying a new car, and your wife wants to buy that little place on Lake Michigan that she has always dreamed about, and you take your adult children and their families on a vacation. Then you go to a financial planner who asks what your income looks like and you say "Nothing. I just sold my business 6 months ago."

It is not uncommon knowledge that professional athletes have a tendency to go broke. The world seems baffled and appalled by the fact that these gladiators that entertained them for years while earning multi-million dollar contracts could be put in a position to declare bankruptcy. While we can get into a breakdown of the poor financial decisions that these athletes make while they are still competing, it is undeniable that more often than not, these athletes are trying to live the same lifestyle in retirement as they did when they were in their prime. The problem is they are no longer getting $5,000,000 signing bonuses and 6-figure game checks.

The same thing is not uncommon among entrepreneurs. While the numbers on the checks might be reduced and the opulence of the spending might be less, after the sale of their business there is not a reduction in lifestyle. In fact, as alluded to above, sometimes that payday of the transaction comes in and they take their lifestyle up a notch.

This is not to say that the sale of your business should not be celebrated or that you cannot fund your retirement from the proceeds of a sale. I am not even going to try and say that you need to hold out and be sure that you build your business to the point where a sale is guaranteed to fund your retirement. Planning is the key. Having conversations with experts and professionals that can give you a clear vision of what you need to retire.

The sale of your business might not be enough to fund your retirement but no one said that the sale of your business had to be the end. As pointed out earlier, you probably are going to want to dabble in something business related anyway. If the sale of your business gets you out of the grind, allows you to work less than 10 hours a week on things you see as fun projects and live a lifestyle that you love, why wait for another opportunity? You just have to be fiscally responsible.

PART VI

NOW WHAT

Many of the great producers of our time credit their success to being able to focus on the few areas that can really bring immense value to their business. Warren Buffet says that he says *no* 99 times out of a 100 because those requests for his time and energy are not his priorities. Sir Richard Branson has been willing to walk away from a blank check for his time because motivational speaking was not where he brought his value. Joel Osteen dedicates 5 of the 6 days that he works focused on one task and leaves the rest for his team to handle. Darren Hardy limits what he is willing to do to only three things. Dr. Mehmet Oz says that you need to focus on the vital few functions that make a difference. And Dr. Oz is a guy who is a professor, has a radio show, has a television show, writes books, runs a couple of non-profits and still has time to do 100s of open heart surgeries every year.

There is overwhelming evidence that in order to push your business to greatness, you need to narrow your focus. You have to ask yourself, "Is my true talent creating a sellable entity?" I am going to guess most of you are going to say *no* because you very well would not be reading this book if one of the things you are really great at is creating businesses that are ready to be sold. If creating a sellable business was what you were great at, you probably would have already written your own book educating business owners on the process.

There is a good chance even with the information in this book you still do not know what step one is let alone if you are anywhere near ready to sell your business. You need help! Visit this book's companion website, www.SellSmallBiz.com. There you can find supplemental materials, how to find the right advisers and more. You can even receive a free assessment of your business that allows you to see where your business stands today.

The worst thing you can do is stick this book up on a shelf and forget about it. Having this book sitting around doesn't actually accomplish anything. You have to go out and execute. Even if you don't know how to do that, get someone in your inner circle that does. Get someone who is going to push you to take actions and who is going to support you. You already know you want things to be different. If you are reading this you know they can be different. But doing the same thing as you have been doing isn't going to get the job done. Then in a few years you are going to catch a news story about the guy down the street that sold his business for millions of dollars and he is 15 years younger than you are. Don't be the one reading that story. Be that story. And it starts today.

Best of luck to all those that have made it this far. I know greatness is in all of you. It's a matter of you unlocking it and proving to the world that you have a legacy that is worth preserving.

ABOUT THE AUTHOR

Andrew Longcore was raised in West Michigan and following his graduation from Michigan State University he attended Thomas M. Cooley Law School in Grand Rapids, Michigan. Andrew graduated from law school with a concentration in business transactions.

Andrew founded The Business Law Group in 2012 with the express purpose of serving small and medium size business owners achieve their maximum potential. Based on the premise that legal services should be secondary to valuable business counsel, The Business Law Group serves as partner to many Michigan businesses and business owners.

Married with three children, Andrew serves the West Michigan community as a member of numerous nonprofit boards and serves in local government.

To find out more about Andrew, The Business Law Group or other publications by Andrew, visit www.BusinessLawGR.com.

Scan this code with your phone
visit www.sellsmallbiz.com

Made in the USA
Middletown, DE
30 July 2016